My First Acrostic

Young Poets

Edited by Mark Richardson

First published in Great Britain in 2009 by:
Young Writers

Young Writers
Remus House
Coltsfoot Drive
Peterborough
PE2 9JX
Telephone: 01733 890066
Website: www.youngwriters.co.uk

SB ISBN 978-1-84924-674-3

Foreword

The 'My First Acrostic' collection was developed by Young Writers specifically for Key Stage 1 children. The poetic form is simple, fun and gives the young poet a guideline to shape their ideas, yet at the same time leaves room for their imagination and creativity to begin to blossom.

Due to the young age of the entrants we have enjoyed rewarding their effort by including as many of the poems as possible. Our hope is that seeing their work in print will encourage the children to grow and develop their writing skills to become our poets of tomorrow.

Young Writers has been publishing children's poetry for over 19 years. Our aim is to nurture creativity in our children and young adults, to give them an interest in poetry and an outlet to express themselves. This latest collection will act as a milestone for the young poets and one that will be enjoyable to revisit again and again.

Contents

The Poems

Seaside

Sun reflecting on the sand.
Eating ice cream on the sand.
A crab in the sea.
Soft sand on the beach.
Ice cream eating because we are hungry.
Delightful swimming in the deep sea.
Eating burgers on the sand.

Kylie de Carteret (7)
Amherst Primary School, Guernsey

Seaside

Sun shining high in the sky.
Eating ice cream in cones.
A big sandcastle.
Sunny days at the beach.
I like making sandcastles, the biggest one of all.
Digging a big hole.
Enjoying fun in the sun.

Rhiannon Lambert (6)
Amherst Primary School, Guernsey

Seaside

Swimming in the sea
Eating ice creams
Ants on the sand climbing up me
Sitting on the stones
Ice creams splat everywhere
Dancing on the sand
Eating fresh, cold food.

Louise Bullock (6)
Amherst Primary School, Guernsey

Seaside

S unny, blue sky days at the beach.
E ating yummy cold ice cream on the sand.
A nnoyed by chattering, arguing children.
S itting under the bright blue sunny sky.
I played with a beach ball.
D igging a deep hole in the sand.
E ating a hot dog on a deckchair.

Logan Le Messurier (7)
Amherst Primary School, Guernsey

Seaside

Satisfying sun
Excited sandcastles
Amusing swimming
Singing parents
Independent me
Delightful shells
Excellent waves.

Eleanor Batiste (7)
Amherst Primary School, Guernsey

Seaside

S uper sandcastles
E xcellent swimming
A mazed people
S inging babies because they like the beach
I ce creams melting
D isco on the beach
E xcited children because they like the beach.

Naomi Sanga (7)
Amherst Primary School, Guernsey

Seaside

Sunny day at the beach.
Eating ice cream, that's a treat.
Amazing shells.
Satisfying swimming.
Ice cream time.
Delightful food.
Exciting surfing.

Chelsea Kinney (7)
Amherst Primary School, Guernsey

Holidays

Happy
Open top bus
Lobsters
Igloos in cold places
Ducks on the pond
Around the world
Yellow sun
Summer.

Mia Crellin (6)
Anagh Coar Primary School, Isle of Man

Holidays

Hot sand
Over the sea
Laying on the beach
Ice cream
Dig a hole
A sunny day
Yellow sun
Sandcastles.

Kane Munn-Mingins (6)
Anagh Coar Primary School, Isle of Man

Holidays

H appy
O n a plane
L ay down on the sand
I ce cream
D ig a hole
A round the world
Y ellow sun
S andcastles.

Ryan Coleman (6)
Anagh Coar Primary School, Isle of Man

Holidays

Hot beach
Octopus in the sea
Laugh
Ice lollies
Dig a hole
Around the world
Yellow sand
Seaside.

Kyra Campbell (6)
Anagh Coar Primary School, Isle of Man

Holidays

H appy
O tter spotting in the water
L ovely sunny days
I ce lollies on the beach
D og on the beach
A round the world
Y oghurt for supper
S eaweed.

Amy Quayle (6)
Anagh Coar Primary School, Isle of Man

Holidays

Happy
Octopus
Lobster
Ice lolly
Days out
Adventures
Yellow sunshine
Sand in your pants.

Jamie Blayden (6)
Anagh Coar Primary School, Isle of Man

Holidays

Hot sun
On the sea
Lobster
Ice lolly
Duck on the pond
Adventures
Yellow sand
Summer.

Brandon O'Neill (6)
Anagh Coar Primary School, Isle of Man

Holidays

Happy
Open top bus
Laugh
Ice cream
Dig a hole
Around the world
Yoghurts for lunch
Sunny day.

Tia Brennan (6)
Anagh Coar Primary School, Isle of Man

Seaside

S easides are very rocky
E veryone has fun
A eroplanes are twirling in the air
S easides are sandy
I ce creams are cold
D ogs are running on the beach
E at chips with gravy.

Chantelle Taggart (7)
Anagh Coar Primary School, Isle of Man

Holidays

Holidays are sunny
On holidays people like to go paddling
Lovely games to play
Ice cream is dripping onto the sand
Dripping down my arm
At night-time it's cold
Yachts are bobbing on the sea
Shining on the water.

Carly Skillen (7)
Anagh Coar Primary School, Isle of Man

easide

S easides are rocky
E very day the sun shines
A ll the children have ice cream
S easide is very, very hot
I ce cream is very, very cold and very, very tasty
D elicious ice cream on my tongue
E veryone loves the seaside.

Amy Playford (7)
Anagh Coar Primary School, Isle of Man

Holidays

Holidays are cool
On the beach you can have fun
Lots of ice creams
I love ice cream when I eat one
Days can be different
Aeroplanes fly over everybody
Years go past, summer's here
Seagulls spread their wings.

Scott Elson (7)
Anagh Coar Primary School, Isle of Man

Seaside

S easides are rocky
E verybody likes the beach
A eroplanes are above
S ea is splashing roughly
I ce cream is yummy
D on't forget the Flake!
E verybody is hot.

Tyler Dunsmore (7)
Anagh Coar Primary School, Isle of Man

Seaside

S easides are sunny
E ach person has an ice cream
A eroplanes are flying
S ome children are walking on the beach
I ce creams are yummy
D ogs are running
E at your ice creams before they melt.

James Crellin (6)
Anagh Coar Primary School, Isle of Man

Seaside

S easides are sandy
E very day is sunny
A ll the rocks are soggy
S ometimes people play with balls
I ce cream is dripping
D ogs are running fast
E very day people play in the cold water.

Takara Brennan (7)
Anagh Coar Primary School, Isle of Man

Holidays

Holidays are fun
Orange fish
Lots of shells
International aeroplanes go past
Drinks are fizzy
A race goes on
You can have fun
Sea to paddle in.

Glenn Boland (6)
Anagh Coar Primary School, Isle of Man

Holidays

Holidays are fun.
Out on a sunny day.
Lots of ice cream is nice.
I love ice cream.
Days out are funny.
A beautiful day.
You would like a sunny day.
Sunny days are hot.

Kerrie Guttridge (7)
Anagh Coar Primary School, Isle of Man

Elephant

Eats apples
Love their mummy
Eat some berries
Pull a rope
Hold their trunks
Ants
Not afraid
They are lovely.

Lorraine Wormald (5)
Callington Primary School, Callington

Cheetah

C at
H unter
E ating
E nergetic
T hey eat meat
A ction
H unts for food.

Alex Hooker (5)
Callington Primary School, Callington

Tiger

Terror
In the jungle
Great
Eat me
Run.

Connor McCullum (5)
Callington Primary School, Callington

Squirrel

S mall
Q uick
U nafraid
I t can jump
R attling
R uns fast
E ating nuts
L ong tail.

Josie Pethick (5)
Callington Primary School, Callington

Bottle

Breakable when it's glass
Orange ones can be for fizzy juice
Tall bottles
Thin bottles
Look through them when they are glass
Eggs can't be in bottles.

Max Pawley (5)
Callington Primary School, Callington

Tyrannosaurus

T rampling
Y ellow eyes
R unning
A ngry
N oisy
N ot friendly
O range
S ad
A predator, chasing its prey
U pset
R oaring
U gly
S oft.

Callum Slater (6)
Callington Primary School, Callington

Lion

Lying in the sun.
In the pride.
On the hunt.
Never afraid.

Zachary Stribley (6)
Callington Primary School, Callington

Fish

F in
I n the sea
S wimming
H iding.

Shannon Burstow (6)
Callington Primary School, Callington

Rabbit

Run
After it runs it has its food.
Balls you can get from pet shops.
Balls are made for rabbits.
In the field it eats grass.
Try to pull the food off each other.

Hannah Rundle (6)
Callington Primary School, Callington

Star

Star in the sky
Twinkling
A star
Really twinkling.

Megan Maby (6)
Callington Primary School, Callington

Sam

Smiles
Apples are nice
Makes play dough.

Sam Elford (6)
Callington Primary School, Callington

Holly

Helpful Holly,
Octopus are my favourite,
Likes love,
Lovely lollies,
Yellow is my house colour.

Holly Kitchen (6)
Callington Primary School, Callington

James

Jolly James
Apples are best
My moose is colourful
Eggs are yuck
Snakes are slimy.

James Slater (6)
Callington Primary School, Callington

Bethany

Bethany eats bananas
Emily is my sister
Tiny
Happy
Always helpful
Needs help sometimes
Yoghurts are my favourite food.

Bethany Cook (6)
Callington Primary School, Callington

lEva Pascoe

Eats chips
Violins are my favourite
Apples are my favourite

Perfect Eva
Ana is my sister
Splits I like doing
Chickens I've got
Octopus are my favourite
Eva is my name.

Eva Pascoe (6)
Callington Primary School, Callington

Adelle

Adelle eats apples
Dancer
Eats eggs
Loves animals
Loves Daddy
Eats toast.

Adelle Court (6)
Callington Primary School, Callington

Bethany

Bethany likes beans.
Eats eggs.
Teeth are shiny.
Hat on her head.
A good girl.
Nanny likes me.
Yo-yos are fun.

Bethany Greenwood (6)
Callington Primary School, Callington

Sharks In The Ocean!

Sharp teeth like a pirate's knife!
Help, I'm being attacked by a . . . human!
Am I scary or what?
Really gloomy, frightening eyes and enormous scary body!
Killing fish by chewing and munching them all up!

Faye Wyatt (7)
Charborough Road CP School, Bristol

Dolphins Poem

Dolphins jump as high as the sky
out of the deep blue sea!

Ocean is my home, though it is very deep and gloomy!

Lovely land is always far away for
any animals that live under the salty sea.

Pictures of me are sometimes found in a museum.

Help me and the other dolphins, we are in danger
there is pollution about!

I am not scary! Trust me, I do not eat you!

Natural, nature look after it please, I'll love you!

Hannah Goddard (7)
Charborough Road CP School, Bristol

Jellyfish

Jellyfish can sting you.
Every day jellyfish swim.
Look at fish swim.
Lovely and colourful.
You can't catch one.
Fish are scared of them.
It is dark under the sea.
Scared of sharks.
Hiding behind a reef.

Cerys Hilton (6)
Charborough Road CP School, Bristol

Shark

Sharks have teeth.
Have sharks got big teeth?
Are fish scared of sharks?
Really dangerous.
Keep away from sharks!

Annabelle Thomas (6)
Charborough Road CP School, Bristol

Dolphins

Dolphins are very beautiful.
Octopus are scared of dolphins.
Lollies are dolphins' favourite food.
Pipes of water fill up the sea.
Hector is a dolphin as well.
It's a very, very nice animal.
Never hurts people or other sea creatures.
Sea is where dolphins live.

Skye McCrimmond (6)
Charborough Road CP School, Bristol

Whale

Water comes out of their blowhole
Have a big hump on their back
Are whales nasty?
Look out!
Eat lots of fish.

Samuel Brookman (6)
Charborough Road CP School, Bristol

Whale

Whales make loud noises.
Have a big tail.
And they've got little teeth.
Little face.
Eggs in his tummy.

Dalal Al-Bairami (5)
Charborough Road CP School, Bristol

Lightsaber

Light moving quickly through the air.
Igniting the night.
Gradually winning duels.
Hitting blade to blade.
They are really cool.
Silently passing through the air.
A big blade of light.
Bringing peace to the galaxy.
Evil kneels before it.
Running through flesh.

Isaac Humphries (7)
Dover Park Primary School, Isle of Wight

In The Waves

In the sea is fun, fun
Near the fish is bubbly fun

The jellyfish plays
He tickles you
Everybody found a treasure chest.

Where did it come from?
A crab lands splat in the sand
Vicky swam past
Excited about the find
See the bubbly fun.

Rosie Bradshaw (7)
Dover Park Primary School, Isle of Wight

Spider-Man

Spider-Man fights baddies
People cheer for him
I think he is great
Demons and monsters fight him
Evil people hate him
Really friendly man he is
-
Men want to be him
Aliens fight him
No baddy beats him.

Joseph Boulter (7)
Dover Park Primary School, Isle of Wight

TARDIS

Time machine
At lots of planets
Rough wooden building
Down to new time
It arrives
Safely on the ground.

Nicholas Phythian (7)
Dover Park Primary School, Isle of Wight

Lion

Loud roars.
Invincible lions are.
Opening eyes.
Not a single leaf in its mouth.

George Foulsham (7)
Dover Park Primary School, Isle of Wight

Lego

Little pieces
Every part fixes together
Great fun
Opening and closing Lego doors.

Jake Mills (7)
Dover Park Primary School, Isle of Wight

Tiger

Telling young what to do
Ill and better
Going out, hunting at night for its prey
Even happier today
Really good and healthy.

Faith Western (7)
Dover Park Primary School, Isle of Wight

Binka

Binka is a lazy cat
Indoors he will stay lazy
No one stops him loving Sukey
Kneeling down when he sleeps
Afternoons he dreams of fish.

Ezme Skinner (7)
Dover Park Primary School, Isle of Wight

Snake

Slithery snake that bounces
Natural body that's thin
A circle head so slimy
Kind spotty snake
Eating in the forest snake.

Sianli Pelling (7)
Dover Park Primary School, Isle of Wight

Teddy

The funny teddy
Eats lots of food
Dobby is her name
Dinosaurs are her favourite thing
Yawns a lot.

Bailey Julian (7)
Dover Park Primary School, Isle of Wight

Polar Bear

P olar bear, polar bear lives
O n the ice and hunts
L ow and high for seals and fish.
A dd more polar bears, add more polar bears.
R oar, roar polar bears go roar, roar.

B ite, bite on the seals and fish
E ating seals and fish and feeding its babies
A nd feeding itself
R un, run to its prey.

Elijah Farr-Bishop (7)
Dover Park Primary School, Isle of Wight

Doctor Who

Doctor has a TARDIS
One of his sonic screwdrivers has lights
Carries friends into space
Time Lord
Often has adventures
Runs lots

Wears glasses
Hero
Over time he changes.

Nirusan Nimulan (7)
Dover Park Primary School, Isle of Wight

Teacher

Teaching children in classrooms
Eating lunch in the dining room
Always the right question
Call the register
Having long playtime after lunch
Every day they're marking books
Right about everything.

Jade Locke (7)
Dover Park Primary School, Isle of Wight

Lego

L ots of it
E xciting bits
G reat fun
O pening and closing Lego doors.

Joanne Hemming (7)
Dover Park Primary School, Isle of Wight

Kitten Chasing A Butterfly

Kitten chasing a butterfly
In the garden
Then a mouse catches her eye
The mouse scrambles for safety, cat still chasing it
Escaping as the kitten puts her paw down
Night falls and the kitten goes home to bed.

Aeryn Bond (7)
Dover Park Primary School, Isle of Wight

Whale

Wacky and wonderful
Has 3m long flippers
Always swimming
Likes to eat plankton
Energetic mammals
Singing creature.

Stefan Mamula (7)
Dover Park Primary School, Isle of Wight

Robot

Robot rot, rot it goes
Old toy robot it is broken
Bad robot toy
Ouch it says
Toy robot is evil.

Owen Cotton (7)
Dover Park Primary School, Isle of Wight

Lego

L ots of it
E xciting bits of it
G reat people
O pening and closing.

Sonny Wallace (7)
Dover Park Primary School, Isle of Wight

Lion King

Large mane
It lives on a green island
Over the sea
Noble king of the jungle

Killing his prey
In his cave
Napping lion
Growling!

Jay Clasper (7)
Dover Park Primary School, Isle of Wight

Panda

P oor panda
A lways hungry
N early extinct
D ark black and white panda
A bamboo eater.

Alfy Kensit (7)
Dover Park Primary School, Isle of Wight

Dolphin

D olphin shh, dolphin shh stop
O cean roar, sound of music from the sea
L ive and happy
P roud and glad
H appy dolphin
I n the ocean
N ever stop jumping.

Violet Wray (7)
Dover Park Primary School, Isle of Wight

Horse

H arsh riders giving signals
O nly one horse in its stable
R ainbows shining when horses are galloping
S hining horses in the sun
E ating hay for their snack.

Hannah de Grey-Warter (6)
Fowey Primary School, Cornwall

Monkey

Muttering babies all the time
On the move
Nibbling a banana
Kingdom of monkeys
Eating all the time
Yawning all the day.

Jamie Stanlake (6)
Fowey Primary School, Cornwall

Clowns

Cheering people
Loudly clapping
Orange costume
White face paint
Noses honking
Silly clowns.

Hollie Morgan-Rutt (6)
Hemington Primary School, Bristol

Africa

Amazing African anteaters.
Ferocious fighting lions.
Rude rhinos roaming around making a racket.
Incredibly interesting iguanas.
Chattering cheetahs.
Africa amazement.

Tom Stapley (7)
La Houguette Primary School, Guernsey

Amazing Africa

Amazing animals in Africa.
Fantastic flying flamingos everywhere.
Rude rhinos butting you around.
Incredible colourful indigo.
Cheetahs running everywhere nearly knocking you over!
Africa is the best!

Louis Naftel (6)
La Houguette Primary School, Guernsey

Africa

Astonishing birds flying high
Female flamingos flapping around
Rude rhinos running round
Incredible insects you find in the grass
Curious camels carrying cargo
Africa is just the best.

Alexandra Oliver (7)
La Houguette Primary School, Guernsey

Africa

Amazing animals all around.
Flying flamingos with fantastic feathers.
Rude rhinos running round.
Incredible insects in indigo
Colourful and cool camels.
Apes are in Africa.

Daniel Collenette (6)
La Houguette Primary School, Guernsey

Africa

Amazing animals that live in Africa.
Fabulous fish that are made out of pottery.
Rocks are in rivers all bumpy and hard.
Incredible iguanas with indigo scales.
Colourful crabs all creamy and white.
A is for Africa with a really big heart.

Jaimie Paige Sheppard (7)
La Houguette Primary School, Guernsey

Africa

Amazing African animals
Fierce, fresh, flapping fish.
Rivers rushing.
Incredible indigo iguanas.
Colourful crabs.
Astonishing anteaters.

Rosa Bonner-Morgan (6)
La Houguette Primary School, Guernsey

Africa

Amazing animals in Africa.
Fresh, fantastic fruit.
Rugged rocks rushing.
Infecting insects.
Cool, colourful crabs.
Africa is amazing.

Lydia Symphorien (7)
La Houguette Primary School, Guernsey

Africa

A mazing African animals
F ierce flapping fish
R ushing rivers
I ncredible insects
C ool cats catching crabs
A stonishing anteaters.

William Mahy (7)
La Houguette Primary School, Guernsey

Africa

Amazing birds can fly high.
Fast cheetahs can run faster than a lizard.
Ripe fruit is on the trees.
Incredible lizards live in Africa.
Curious elephants have huge tusks.
Amazing anteater.

Lily Inniss (7)
La Houguette Primary School, Guernsey

Africa

A rchaeologists in Africa.
F resh, fantastic fish.
R iver rushing fast.
I nsects flying.
C ool cats are in a jungle.
A mazing animals in Africa.

Jordan Robins (7)
La Houguette Primary School, Guernsey

Africa

Amazing African animals
Fierce fish swimming fast
Rhinos running on the rocks
Incredible indigo insects
Crabs on the yellow sand of the continent
Astonishing anteaters.

Jennifer Thomas (7)
La Houguette Primary School, Guernsey

Africa

A mazing ants.
F at hippos in the water.
R ats running out of houses.
I ntelligent wise people.
C rocodiles cutting crabs with their teeth.
A nteaters eating ants.

Harry Phillips (7)
La Houguette Primary School, Guernsey

Amazing Africa

Amazing African animals.
Flapping fish.
Rough rhinos.
Interesting insects.
Cool kittens.
Angry animals.

Eve Bott (6)
La Houguette Primary School, Guernsey

Africa

African deserts waiting to be found
Flamingos in the lake with only one foot on the ground
Rude rhinos in the mud
I am fascinated by all the flower buds
Cunning animals in the trees
Africa is just great to me!

Daisy Whiteman (7)
La Houguette Primary School, Guernsey

Sports Day

Saturday sports day
People putting
Obstacles down, children
Ready to go.
Try their best for their team.
Still going fast.

Dying to win the race.
Adults,
Yelling for their children, 'You've won!'

Naomi Flux (7)
Mylor Bridge Community Primary School, Cornwall

Sports Day

Sun was shining, it was very hot.
People running down the lanes.
Over to Mr Lea to get their stickers.
Red group running as fast as they could
to get to the finish line.
The sun was getting hotter every second.
Some dads ran.

Day is fun.
All the children were laughing.
Yes the day is done.

Grace Mayer (7)
Mylor Bridge Community Primary School, Cornwall

Sports Day

Sun was very hot.
People were winning different races.
Over the line everyone runs.
Racing all day long.
The dads were running very fast.
So hot everyone became.

Day was fun.
All the people were cheering.
Yellow team didn't win.

Ciara Benny (7)
Mylor Bridge Community Primary School, Cornwall

Sports Day

Sprinting was my favourite race.
People were cheering for children.
Over the obstacles.
Red team tried to win.
Teams tried to do their best.
Skipping I came first.

Daddies did a race as well.
And we got sweaty.
Young people had lots of fun.

Ione Wild (7)
Mylor Bridge Community Primary School, Cornwall

Oak Tree

Oak tree, oak tree getting hot in the sun, cold in the wind.
An owl sat in the tree hooting in the wind, rivers running,
never stopping, never ever, ever stopping.
Keep going, always winding, never stopping, never stopping.

Trees leaves swaying, swaying, swaying.
Really loud the cars come rushing down the road,
twisting and bending around the corners.
Everlasting, the road coming up the hill, going down again.
Evening time the oak tree went quiet.

James Lansdowne (7)
Mylor Bridge Community Primary School, Cornwall

Oak Tree

Over on an island there stood an oak tree.
In the sea came a boat.
Afternoon came and the oak tree saw that he had company.
Kookaburra came with his kookaburra friends.

Two owls were up on the oak tree.
Rabbits came running.
Eagles flew past
Evening came and night.

Alistair Mantle (7)
Mylor Bridge Community Primary School, Cornwall

Oak Tree

Over a hillside there grew an oak tree.
Autumn arrived and the oak tree lost its leaves.
Koalas climbed the tree each day.

The oak tree felt acorns growing on its twigs.
Rabbits hopped past the tree.
Evening came and the tree felt sleepy.
Evening came and everything was quiet.

Annie Trenoweth (6)
Mylor Bridge Community Primary School, Cornwall

Tamsin

Toast with jam is my favourite breakfast
Always playing hide-and-seek
My cats are called Molly and Cubix
Silly games with my friends
I love my purple bedroom
Nearly late every day for school.

Tamsin Sanders (7)
Pondhu Primary School, Cornwall

Corbin

Clumsy when I'm walking
Only allowed to play in my room
Run fast on sports day
Best at moving my eyebrows
I love drawing robots
Nearly completed my Transformers game.

Corbin Varker (7)
Pondhu Primary School, Cornwall

Chloe

Cute, cuddly and extremely smart
Happy to help your friends
Laughing at my dad's jokes
Oh I would love to be a pop star
Excited when it is my seventh birthday.

Chloe Tyrrell (6)
Pondhu Primary School, Cornwall

Rebecca

Really silly when people joke
Extremely happy to be a bridesmaid
Baby brothers are such hard work
Excited on my seventh birthday
Clever at drawing
Clever at lots of things
Adorable when I wear my best dresses.

Rebecca Gregory (7)
Pondhu Primary School, Cornwall

Heather

H appy when I get a cuddle from Dad.
E xcited when my nan comes round.
A pples are my favourite fruit.
T offee is a delicious sweet.
H ot days I like to run in the sun.
E legant when I don't want to play.
R unning down the road in the rain.

Heather Brandon (7)
Pondhu Primary School, Cornwall

Charlie

Cricket is my favourite sport to play
Harvey, my beautiful black Labrador, likes to lick me
America was the best holiday ever
Reliable with my friends
Laying on my bed and listening to the pirate song
I am a cheeky monkey
Easter is my most exciting time of the year.

Charlie Haining (7)
Pondhu Primary School, Cornwall

Sam

S pain is my favourite holiday place.
A lways funny when I run around like crazy.
M y sister Mollie-Jean is a little monkey.

Sam Smith (7)
Pondhu Primary School, Cornwall

Bethany

B utlins is my favourite place
E xcited when I go to a diner
T asty treats from Granny Joy
H elp my nan with the shopping
A pples are my favourite fruit
N anny is the best nan ever
Y ellow is the colour of the sun.

Bethany Grant (7)
Pondhu Primary School, Cornwall

Angelina

Adorable when I have my sparkling, pretty dresses on.
Natter on the carpet is what I do.
Great at drawing interesting landscapes.
Excited when I try the 'Freak Out' at the funfair.
Laughing out loud at my birthday party with all my friends.
Ice cream I love when it's a hot day
especially delicious strawberry.
Necklaces I wear to parties to make me look gorgeous.
Always happy when I'm dancing at the disco
in my cool clothes.

Angelina Martin (7)
Pondhu Primary School, Cornwall

Aaliyha

A ugust is my 7th birthday.
A lways happy when I go out for dinner.
L aughing at my mum's jokes.
I ce cream to cool down when it is a hot day.
Y esterday I played with my sister.
H appy when I go to a disco and parties.
A dorable when I say please.

Aaliyha Patton (6)
Pondhu Primary School, Cornwall

Nile

Nearly eight on September 7th
I love going on holiday to Disneyland
Laughing at juggling clowns in the circus
Excited when I'm off to Legoland.

Nile Moore (7)
Pondhu Primary School, Cornwall

Ryan

Really good at maths.
Yucky when I splash in mud at home.
Angry when I don't get a DVD on at home.
Never be loud in the classroom.

Ryan Gale (7)
Pondhu Primary School, Cornwall

Peter

P erfect writing in my spellings
E xcited when I play with the Lego
T asty chicken pie for my tea
E njoy riding my scooter
R unning fast with my friends.

Peter Earl (7)
Pondhu Primary School, Cornwall

Harry J Best

Happy when I'm on Freecycle.
Angry when my brother is mean to me.
Really ace at computers.
Running is my favourite sport.
Yappy when I see Charles and Charlie.

January the 17th is when I will be eight.

Best when I'm at home with my laptop.
Excited when listening to 'Three Days Grace'.
St Austell is where I live.
Trains are my favourite transport.

Harry Best (7)
Pondhu Primary School, Cornwall

Amber

Always happy to help my friend
My friends make me laugh all the time
Bouncing crazily on the trampoline
Excited when I get surprises
Running along the soft sand at the beach.

Amber Nixon (7)
Pondhu Primary School, Cornwall

Charles

Cycling is my favourite sport.
Hary Best is my best friend.
Accurate when I'm doing maths.
Robert is my brother's name.
Laughing at my brother when he is being funny.
Excited when I'm with Harry Best.
St Austell is where I live.

Charles Hocking (7)
Pondhu Primary School, Cornwall

Sandcastle

Shrimp in the big rock pool
A boy buried his dad in the sand
'Nice day,' I said to my mum
Do you want to swim today?
Castle competition on the beach
A bad boy was swimming in the sea
Seagull took my ice cream
Turtle swimming in the ocean
Lifeboat going to rescue someone
Eels have fierce teeth and jaws.

James Sullivan (7)
Rushen Primary School, Isle of Man

Sandcastle

Splashing in the cold sea
All my best friends are at the beach
Naughty seagulls take everyone's sandwiches
Donkeys take people for a ride
Cold ice cream at the ice cream shop
A Flake is in my ice cream
Sunbathing in the sun
Talking to all my friends
Licking my ice lolly
Eating my lunch.

Megan Lockwood (7)
Rushen Primary School, Isle of Man

Sandcastle

Swimming in the blue sea
And making lovely sea pictures in the sand
Nice sandy sandwiches
Dinner on the beach
Collecting shells on the beach
Alex is burying me on the beach
Splashing in the sea
Talking to your friends
Lifeboats coming to the rescue
Elise and Evan jumping over the waves.

Elise Messenger (7)
Rushen Primary School, Isle of Man

Sandcastle

Swimming in the blue sea
And having nice ice cream
No one is allowed in the sea
Dylan jumping in the sea
Castle building, it was big
A wave was really big
Sunny on the beach
Talking to my mum eating ice cream
Lee jumped in the sea
Elley can swim.

Lee McFee (5)
Rushen Primary School, Isle of Man

Sandcastle

Seawater in my wellies
Anemones stick to rocks
Naughty seagulls in the sky
Dancing on the beach
Collecting shells
All my friends came
Surfing in the waves
Turtle swimming around
Lifeboats save people in trouble
Eels eating everyone on the beach.

Beth Mosley (6)
Rushen Primary School, Isle of Man

Sandcastle

Swimming in the sea
A nice cold ice cream
New clothes to wear
Dolphins swim in the sea
Catching fish is good fun
Alex walking on the beach
Saw a basking shark
Talking on the beach to your friends
Lifeboats save people
Emily and Olivia are playing on the beach.

Olivia Leggate (7)
Rushen Primary School, Isle of Man

Sandcastle

Sandwiches covered in sand
A big lifeboat set out to sea
Naughty jellyfish stinging people
Doing water pistol fights
Catching crabs in rock pools
Anemones sticking to wide rocks
Ships going out to sea
Turtles swimming in the sea
Licking cold ice cream
Everyone eating fish.

Django Kinley (7)
Rushen Primary School, Isle of Man

Sandcastle

S and is really, really soft
A nemones stick to the rocks
N aughty boys bury their dads
D iving in the sea
C ollecting stones and shells
A lot of people on the beach
S plashing in the waves
T alking to my friend on the beach
L ifeboat on the sea to the rescue
E than catching an eel.

Ethan Morrow (7)
Rushen Primary School, Isle of Man

Sandcastle

S and in my sandwiches
A nemones in the rock pools
N aughty children buying T-shirts
D iving for shells in the sea
C old children in the sea
A ll ice cream is nice
S urfing and jumping over the waves
T urtles swimming in the sea
L ying on the hot sand
E veryone eating eels.

Kyle Corrin (7)
Rushen Primary School, Isle of Man

Sandcastle

S and is fun to play in
A ll my mum's friends were at the beach
N ice cold ice cream
D on't take my sandwiches
C alling your friend
A naughty boy playing in the sand
S wimming in the sea
T aking home beautiful shells
L ovely eels to eat
E loise is laying on her mum.

Issy Young (5)
Rushen Primary School, Isle of Man

Sandcastle

Sea is very, very salty
Anemones stick to the rocks
Nice ice cream
Dad gets sunburnt
Collecting big shiny shells
A big eel gets washed up
Soft sand
Turtle in the sea
Lifeboat on the sea
Eels on the beach.

Dylan Rainey (6)
Rushen Primary School, Isle of Man

Sandcastle

S unny day with friends
A nd sea horses in the sea
N aughty boys burying their dads
D onkeys on the beach
C ollecting shells
A shrimp in a rock pool
S urfing in the blue sea
T urtles playing around
L ifeboats rescue people
E van playing with Ethan.

Evan Venus (7)
Rushen Primary School, Isle of Man

Sandcastle

S and in my shoes
A lex and Olivia on the beach
N ew nets for fishing
D igging in the sand
C anoeing in the deep cold sea
A cold ice cream
S andwich munching on the beach
T urtles are very cute
L ifeboats are very safe
E els are twisty and bendy.

Alex Johnston (7)
Rushen Primary School, Isle of Man

Sandcastle

Soft sand on the beach
All my friends on the beach
Nice ice cream on the beach
Donkey rides on the beach
Cold after swimming in the sea
Anemones stick to the rocks
Surfing on the waves
Turtles swimming in the sea
Lifeboats going out to sea
Evan and Zac playing on the beach.

Zac Moughton (7)
Rushen Primary School, Isle of Man

Sandcastles

S hiny sea glass washes up
A long the seashore
N ice calm sea in the summer
D ancing waves, jellyfish, dolphins
C astle building competitions on the sand
A ll day I play on the beach
S urfing on the waves
T urtles walking along the beach
L icking ice lollies
E very castle has a flag
S andcastles washed away by the waves.

James Fishwick & Ben Roberts (6)
Rushen Primary School, Isle of Man

Sandcastles

Sand is fun to play on when it is a sunny day.
All day I play on the beach and build sandcastles.
Nice calm sea in the summer when it is sunny.
Dancing dolphins dancing when the waves come.
Come to build a sandcastle with me.
And now come and play in the sea.
Sand is fun to play on.
The tide comes in at a certain time.
Licking ice lollies, it is an orange one.
Every day I go in the sea, it is cool.
Sand is soft to play on.

Tyla Lewis (7)
Rushen Primary School, Isle of Man

Sandcastles

Shiny glass washes up on the seashore.
A beach ball bouncing on the seashore.
Nice calm sea in the summer.
Dancing jellyfish in the sea.
Castles are great.
All day I play on the beach
Surfing on the waves.
Turtles being born.
Licking ice lollies, I like them.
Every castle has a flag.
Sky diving.

Amy Sellors (6)
Rushen Primary School, Isle of Man

Sandcastles

Sunbathing on the beach.
All fish like swimming in the sea.
Nice calm rock pools
Dancing silly fish.
Castle building with your friends.
All day I go to the beach.
Slimy seaweed on the rocks.
Turtles paddling in the water.
Licking cool pops
Every castle has a flag
Sandcastles are sometimes washed away.

Callum Watterson (7)
Rushen Primary School, Isle of Man

Sandcastles

S and
A ll the time I go to the beach
N ow I will get an ice cream
D ancing jellyfish
C alm sea
A ll day I go to the beach
S andy eyes
T ea at the beach
L icking ice lollies
E at an ice cream
S ea.

Harrison Guy (7)
Rushen Primary School, Isle of Man

Sandcastles

Sitting on the beach building sandcastles.
All day I enjoy building sandcastles.
Never boring it is always fun.
Dolphins dancing in the sea.
Cool ice cream.
All day I play at the beach.
Starfish on the seabeds.
Turtles walking along the beach.
Liking the waves go by.
Every castle I like.
Seeing the jellyfish dancing.

Luke Sharp (7)
Rushen Primary School, Isle of Man

Sandcastles

Shining sea everywhere
All along the sea
Nice cold water,
Dancing dolphins on the waves.
Competitions you can watch
All along the shore,
See people sing and dance
Turtles under the sand
Lying down reading a book
Everyone has fun,
Sailing on a boat looking at the sea.

Toby Crossley (6)
Rushen Primary School, Isle of Man

Sandcastles

Shiny sea glass drifting
Along the seashore
Nice ice cream when I go to the beach
Dancing dolphins on the waves
Castle building is fun
All the time when I go to the beach I have fun
Surfing on the waves
Turtles walking along
Licking ice cream
Every family likes the beach
Sand is very soft.

Jacob Meechan (6)
Rushen Primary School, Isle of Man

Sandcastles

Shiny seashells washed up
All along the shore
Nice ice cream from the ice cream van
Dancing dolphins dancing in the waves
Castle building competitions on the sand all day long
All day I play in the sea
Surfing on the waves
Turtles walking along the beach
Lovely ice cream
Every sandcastle I make has a flag
Seaweed gets washed up ashore.

Emily Challenor (7)
Rushen Primary School, Isle of Man

Sandcastles

Sea is cold when I try to swim in it
All my friends are playing with me
Nice ice cream, I asked for toffee crunch, my favourite
Dancing dolphins, I like riding them
Competitions on the sand, I like them
All day I play on the beach
Slimy seaweed on the rocks
Turtles are dancing on the waves
Licking ice lollies
Every sandcastle has a flag on top
Shells are pretty, they are shiny.

Alicia Hide (7)
Rushen Primary School, Isle of Man

Sandcastles

Shiny sea glass washed up
All along the seashore
Nice ice cream you have there
Delicious
Castle building competitions
All day I play on the beach
Seaweed has got flies on it
The sea is very cold
Licking ice cream
Every castle has a flag
Sandcastles are made from sand.

Caprice Barclay (7)
Rushen Primary School, Isle of Man

Sandcastles

Sandcastles get washed up by the sea.
All along the seashore.
No calm sea in the winter.
Dancing dolphins.
Castle competitions on the beach.
All the time I build sandcastles.
Starfish on the seabed.
Turtles walking along.
Licking ice lollies.
Every sandcastle has a flag.
Shiny sea glass washes up.

Marcus Tyrer (7)
Rushen Primary School, Isle of Man

Sandcastle

Swimming in the sea
A picnic with my mum and dad
'Naughty stop putting sand over me'
Dinner on the beach
Calling for my friends
A jellyfish is what I saw
Sand in my crispies
Tea on the beach
Licking an ice cream
Enjoying the beach.

Max Headley (7)
Rushen Primary School, Isle of Man

Rose

R is for red, black and blue, these are *some* of the colours of roses
O is for 'ow' when you prick your finger on its thorns
S is for sunshine to help them grow
E is for England with a sign of a rose.

Camilla Rose Grady (9)
St Lawrence Primary School, Jersey

Love

Camilla

xxx

Flower Acrostic Poem

Flowers are colourful like a sparkling rainbow
Lovely flowers that smell like lavender
Orchids as white as snow
Water feeding beautiful plants
Enormous flowers growing very tall
Roses as red as blood
So many flowers growing everywhere.

James Perestrelo (8)
St Lawrence Primary School, Jersey

Spring

Showers as beautiful as snow falling
Petals falling from a rose that smells as sweet as a candle
Rain falling from the beautiful blue sky as deep
as the deep blue sea
Ice falling on the cars as cold as an icicle
Nine birds sitting on a wall singing as sweet as a choir
Green grass growing as fast as a rabbit bouncing.

Conan Hughes (8)
St Lawrence Primary School, Jersey

Spring

Snowdrops as cold as ice
Parents fly outside like fireworks, flinging into the sky
Rugs as clean as white after a good spring clean
I cook a quiche at my house, it is like a pastry tart
Newborn chicks pop out of their eggs like the sun
popping up in the morning
Growing flowers and plants, growing as fast as me.

Harry Baker (9)
St Lawrence Primary School, Jersey

Spring

Sky's as blue as sharpies, the hot sun is as shiny as diamonds
Pancakes as yummy as omelettes, baby rabbits as cute puppies
Roses as red as rubies, clouds as white as diamonds
Ingredients for a spring dinner, sea as charming as a horse
on a hot sunny spring day
New baby lambs being born in the fields like running rabbits
Golden flowers all as pretty as the sun on a hot spring day.

Cameron White (8)
St Lawrence Primary School, Jersey

Spring

Silently the clouds float by as quiet as a mouse
Prickly bushes growing fast like a racing car on the track
Rabbits as fluffy as candyfloss
In trees there are squirrels as brown as chocolate
Newborn lambs as white as snow
Grass as green as emeralds.

Jasper Crocker-Kilic (9)
St Lawrence Primary School, Jersey

It's Spring Today

Singing birds sing like choirs of angels,
Parents' flowers blooming like fireworks.
Rabbits having their babies in their warm snug den,
then running like the wind.
In the silent sky clouds as fluffy as candyfloss float by.
Newborn birds getting hungry, crying till their mum
comes home.
Get outside in the garden to play, come on everybody,
it's spring today!

Anna Cotillard (8)
St Lawrence Primary School, Jersey

Spring

Showers as silent as snow
Primroses as pink as lipgloss that my mum wears every day
Rabbits as fluffy as a cloud, that gently floats by
Ivy as green as a lime, that you can put in your drink
to make it tasty
Newly grown flowers as pretty as the showers that shine in the sun
Growing trees that leaves fall off with no noise at all,
as silent as the night-time garden.

Tia Olivia Murray (9)
St Lawrence Primary School, Jersey

Spring

Sunny days as hot as lava as I play peacefully with my sister.
Pines grow as big as a giant, as I stare with interest.
Roses as thorny as pins as I prick my fingers while gardening.
Inky black sky as dark as tar on a rainy day.
Now flowers bloom as beautiful as a jewel, their multicoloured petals so pretty in the moonlight.
Grey-green buds start to open as slow as a snail in the sun.

Charlie Larbalestier (9)
St Lawrence Primary School, Jersey

Spring

Snowdrops as white as snow
Perfectly pink as candyfloss
Roughly chopped grass as green as leaves
I smell daffodils in the morning breeze
New grown blossom as pink as strawberries
Growing flowers as colourful as a spring rainbow.

Lucy Price (9)
St Lawrence Primary School, Jersey

Spring

S howers as grey as the road, they will be blown away by the wind
P icking daffodils as gold as the sun, a warm breeze blows by
R owing down rivers that are as blue as the sky
I roning clothes that are as warm as the sun
N ewborn animals as white as cotton wool and as warm
as the blazing sun
G rass as green as God's plants.

Peter Emmanuel (9)
St Lawrence Primary School, Jersey

Squid

Squid have a back-like sack to carry their babies in,
Quiet a lot of squid look rough but they are actually smooth,
Under the sea, squid hunting for fish,
Inject ink when they're scared but only at other animals,
Deep water is the water that squid like the most so they can
hide and swim.

Sam Burt (7)
Sandford Primary School, Winscombe

Animals

Animals are cute and cuddly
Never go near dangerous ones as they will bite or claw!
In the jungle my favourite animal is a monkey swinging
with a long tail through the trees
Many are becoming extinct as we are using them for jumpers
and coats
Animals need care but wild ones have to take care of themselves
Lions and tigers are very good at hunting their prey
Slithering, climbing, pacing, flying and bouncing, there are
loads of different animals in the world.

Ellis Warman (7)
Sandford Primary School, Winscombe

Seaside

Sand, soft and fun at the seaside
Enjoyable making castles and digging deep holes
All around the beach people laughing and chatting
Strong, wavy waves crashing onto the sharp rocks
Ice cream, frozen and creamy
Deckchairs, bright and stripy
Excited children swimming in the deep blue sea.

Mikey Stam (7)
Sandford Primary School, Winscombe

Sparkly Shells

Shimmery shells on the beach
Perhaps we'll buy ice cream too
A crab in a rock pool scuttling away
Rocks in all colours at the beach today
Kind people let us have a turn of their kite
Let's have fun in the sun today
You and me can make a sandcastle

Sink our toes into the soft sand
How about a swim in the sea?
Eat our picnic with my family
Let's bury my dad while he's asleep
Let's watch a Punch and Judy show
Sometimes I wonder if it's real though.

Keira Mackey (7)
Scoill Vallajeelt, Isle of Man

The Seaside

The seaside is really fun
Have an ice cream at the seaside
Eating at the beach is great

Sometimes the sea is freezing!
Everyone loves the beach
A person borrowing my beach ball
Sunny days are great for the beach
I love the sparkly shells
Dolphins can dive
Everyone wants to go to the beach.

Darcy Thatcher (7)
Scoill Vallajeelt, Isle of Man

Shells

Sunny days on the beach
Heaps and heaps of shells
Everybody comes to play
Lots of fun on a perfect day
Limpits, winkles, cockles too
Starfish, sandcastles for me and you.

Conal Lowry (7)
Scoill Vallajeelt, Isle of Man

The Seaside

The summer's here, jump up and play
Herrings are caught and smoked into kippers
Eating ice creams on the beach

Salty water in the sea
Eat fish and chips on the sand
And fishing boats catching fish
Seagulls flying in the sky
I like to play beach ball
Dogs paddling in the sea
Ends with a sunset.

Joshua Crichton (7)
Scoill Vallajeelt, Isle of Man

The Seaside

The seaside is a sunny place where you can visit
Have fish and chips at teatime
Eat whilst watching the sunset go down

Swimming in the sea is dead fun!
Everyone loves the seaside
A friend wanted to play beach ball with me
Sunny days are nice at the seaside
If you can't swim you can paddle around the beach
Drinking orange juice at the seaside is brill
Enjoy making sandcastles at the beach.

Finn Shimmin (7)
Scoill Vallajeelt, Isle of Man

The Starfish

The starfish sticks to rocks
Hot starfish can go to the sea
Each starfish is different

Starfish have spots on them
There are loads of starfish in the sea
A starfish sticks to glass if it is in our tank
Regrow - if a starfish loses an arm it grows another
Food is digested outside a starfish's body
Is a starfish different? Yes!
Starfish cannot swim
How amazing! Starfish have two stomachs.

Erin Inglis (6)
Scoill Vallajeelt, Isle of Man

Whales And Fish

Whales live in the seas
Herrings are caught and smoked into kippers
A whale's noise echoes in the sea
Listen to a whale's noise if you are a diver
Echoes to be heard all around the shoreline
Shoals of fish to be seen all the time

Angler is a fish I have for my tea
Nice, fresh and tasty just for me
Did you know there is an Atlantic Football Fish?

Frilled sharks look like eels
I watch the rocks and the sound of the seals
Sit and have a picnic, watch the world go by
Hope you enjoyed the poem, goodbye, goodbye.

Danny Marty Scott (7)
Scoill Vallajeelt, Isle of Man

Sea And Sand

See Punch and Judy, listen to a band
Eating a picnic with your feet on the sand
A lovely day out, blue sky and sun

A day to remember, we had so much fun
No rain to spoil things
Donkeys with children trotting by

Sandcastles by boys and girls are made
A wonderful time with our bucket and spade
Next we go paddling in the cold blue sea
Dancing with joy, you and me.

Amy Corlett (7)
Scoill Vallajeelt, Isle of Man

The Seaside

The seaside's really wonderful
Have a bucket and spade to make sandcastles
Eat an ice cream on the beach

Seasides are great
Exciting bands you can watch
A game of ball would be great
See Punch and Judy on the beach
Ice creams are wonderful to eat
Daydreaming on the beach
Entertaining stuff you can watch.

Martha Anne Teare (7)
Scoill Vallajeelt, Isle of Man

The Shells

There are shells on the beach
Here and there people are sunbathing
Everywhere there is sand

Sun shines on the beach in the summer
Have a fun time on the beach
Enjoy the sea while you can
Laugh on the beach
Lick some ice cream
Shells on the beach.

Ciara Butler (7)
Scoill Vallajeelt, Isle of Man

The Beach

The beach is cool as you will see
Holidays are the time for me
Everyone loves the sea

Buckets and spades can be fun
Eating ice cream when it's hot in the sun
A paddle in the sea helps you to keep cool
Castles of sand and rocky pools
How I really love the sea.

Daniel Sowerby (7)
Scoill Vallajeelt, Isle of Man

The Seaside

T alk and walk along the beach
H ave an ice cream on the seaside
E at a picnic on the sand

S wimming in the sea is lots of fun
E xcited children can play all day
A game of beach ball would be fun
S andcastles you can make lots
I like looking in the rock pools
D iving in the sea, can you see?
E ating ice creams are my favourite.

Mia Hall (7)
Scoill Vallajeelt, Isle of Man

The Shells

The beach is so great
Heavy waves are fun
Each day it's great

Shells are cool
Have a break in the sun
Eat an ice cream
Lovely days in the sun
Lovely beaches are the best
Sunny beaches.

Lucas Parker (6)
Scoill Vallajeelt, Isle of Man

The Beach

The people go shrimping
Here comes a boat
Enjoying the sea are the fishes

Beaches are great and amazing
Excited children like to lay there
And they enjoy swimming
Crabs are crawling
Here is the sun shining.

Varun Vipul Chodanker (7)
Scoill Vallajeelt, Isle of Man

The Seaside

The seaside is very cold to swim in
Have a picnic at the beach
Excited children on the beach making sandcastles

Sparkly shells under the soft sand
Everyone is playing in the summer on the beach
Along you walk into the sea
Small scuttling creatures along the sand
I love to play beach ball
Dolphins can jump out of the sea
Enjoying ice creams sitting on the mats.

Gabriella Paul (6)
Scoill Vallajeelt, Isle of Man

The Seaside

The beach is fun to play on
Have an ice cream in the sun
Eating a picnic on the beach

Sunbathe on the sand
Explore a rock pool
Ask for a sandwich
Sit in the sun
Ice cream is yum in my tum
Drink lemonade
Enjoy time in the sun.

Lauren Pope (7)
Scoill Vallajeelt, Isle of Man

The Seaside

The seaside is so much fun
Hiding and playing in the sand
Eating on the hot beach

Swimming in the sea
Excited children playing
A lovely rock pool in the distance
Sea is sparkling
I love the seaside
Diving in the sea
Excited to watch Punch and Judy.

Charlotte Capewell (7)
Scoill Vallajeelt, Isle of Man

The Sea

Turtles swim underwater,
Herrings get caught and smoked,
Excited children play on the beach.

Swimming with the dolphins,
Eat an ice cream on the beach,
A whale sings in the sea.

Luke Strickett-Morling (7)
Scoill Vallajeelt, Isle of Man

The Sea

The sea is very fun!
Hot sun warms the water
Everyone loves the sea

Shells sparkle in the sea
Enormous waves roll
All of us have fun.

Hana Lawrie (6)
Scoill Vallajeelt, Isle of Man

Butterfly

Beautiful spots on their wings
Unusual insects are always wonderful
To see they are amazing
They are also quiet
Everything they touch is magical
Roaring isn't their language, singing is
Flying around the sky with lovely smiles
Luminous butterflies are also beautiful
Yellow butterflies give wishes like a fairy.

Ananya Sanagavaram (7)
The British School of Amsterdam, Amsterdam

Korea

Korea is a good land to go to.
Or Korea is a clean place to live.
Reports are different in Korea.
Everybody in Korea is happy.
All things in Korea are not the same as things in Holland.

Dong Min Kim (7)
The British School of Amsterdam, Amsterdam

Vikings

Vikings are fun.
I like learning about the Vikings.
Killing animals is how they eat, live.
Inside their house it is poor.
Never fight them or you will lose.
Great at sailing.
Sweden is where they come from.

Esther David-Deleplanque (7)
The British School of Amsterdam, Amsterdam

Niamh, My Best Friend

Niamh is extremely nice
Is amazing
Always plays with me
My friend
Has good ideas.

Juliane Hyvert (7)
The British School of Amsterdam, Amsterdam

Happy

Huge smiles
Always pleasant
Perfect mood
Present to all
You have to be happy.

Misaki Okuyama (7)
The British School of Amsterdam, Amsterdam

Spok, A Game I Like To Play

S uper fun
P erfect game
O utstanding
K ing of games.

Sam McLean (6)
The British School of Amsterdam, Amsterdam

Animals

Amazing creatures
Nice
Incredible habitat
Marvellous shape
All very pretty
Lovely and attractive
Soft and also super.

Lucy Van Blanken (7)
The British School of Amsterdam, Amsterdam

Vikings

V ery mean
I ncredibly strong
K ings
I ntelligent
N asty
G iant tummy
S eriously bloodthirsty.

Vrishin Mehta (6)
The British School of Amsterdam, Amsterdam

Motorbikes

Monster masher
Only fast
Top speed
Operates smoothly
Brilliant to race
I like them a lot
King of roads
Everyone likes them
Special to me.

Federico Mariani (7)
The British School of Amsterdam, Amsterdam

Sarah, My Baby Sister

S oft skin
A mazing
R eally cute
A lready smiling
H appy smile.

Emily Turner (7)
The British School of Amsterdam, Amsterdam

Milo

My name is Milo!
I love dragons
Love to daydream and never do work at home
Over the mountain top in a cave is *me!*

Miles Marchiori (7)
The British School of Amsterdam, Amsterdam

Polina

Peaches, *mmm*, red and round, very yummy in my mouth!
Open swimming pools are great
Love to sing and dance
In the land of wonder
Nits! Disgusting, I hate them
Animals are all my friends.

Polina Kleandrova (7)
The British School of Amsterdam, Amsterdam

Thor

Thor is a Viking
He loves goat to eat
On a summer holiday
Roar, a big roar.

Gregor Wenman (7)
The British School of Amsterdam, Amsterdam

Stars

S hiny stars in the sky
T winkling stars twinkling around
A ll the stars are still in the sky
R eally look up in the night sky
S tars light up the night sky.

Jennifer Hamlyn (7)
Tregadillett Community Primary School, Cornwall

Stars

Shiny stars
Twinkly stars
All of the stars are racing around
Race every night
Stars are bright.

Kyle Sandercock (7)
Tregadillett Community Primary School, Cornwall

Stars

Shiny super stars
Twinkling stars
Always shiny
Rising backwards
Sparkling, lovely stars.

Molly Wood (6)
Tregadillett Community Primary School, Cornwall

Stars

S wirly stars at night
T wirling around the moon
A lways moving, moving around the Earth
R otating everywhere and they never disappear
S tarring the night so quickly.

Jasmin Gill (7)
Tregadillett Community Primary School, Cornwall

Stars

S hiny stars
T winkle like light
A star is bright
R acing rockets through the stars
S tars are there when you can't see them.

Richard Platts (7)
Tregadillett Community Primary School, Cornwall

Stars

Shining around the solar system
Twinkling in every place you go to
Always there, they never go
Racing around planets for long
Still there when it looks like they are not.

Mark Horrell (6)
Tregadillett Community Primary School, Cornwall

Stars

S tars sparkling on their own
T winkling around in space, disappearing
A lways there but you don't think so
R ockets whizzing around
S anta's there in his sleigh at Christmas.

Simon Cornish (7)
Tregadillett Community Primary School, Cornwall

Stars

S pace lights in the air
T winkly stars in space
A ll around space and planets
R acing round the rings
S hiny stars around the air.

Quisha Pearce (6)
Tregadillett Community Primary School, Cornwall

Stars

Sparkly, shiny stars in the sky
Twinkly, twisting stars
All of the stars are around us
Racing rockets in the night
Swirling stars all around us.

Bethany Bell (7)
Tregadillett Community Primary School, Cornwall

Young Writers Information

We hope you have enjoyed reading this book - and that you will continue to enjoy it in the coming years.

If you like reading and writing poetry drop us a line, or give us a call, and we'll send you a free information pack.

Alternatively if you would like to order further copies of this book or any of our other titles, then please give us a call or log onto our website at www.youngwriters.co.uk.

Young Writers Information
Remus House
Coltsfoot Drive
Peterborough
PE2 9JX
(01733) 890066